ANIMAL DANGER ZONE

SHARK!

Willow Clark

WINDMILL
BOOKS

New York

Published in 2011 by Windmill Books, LLC
303 Park Avenue South, Suite # 1280, New York, NY 10010-3657

CREDITS:
Author: Willow Clark
Edited by: Jennifer Way
Designed by: Brian Garvey

Photo Credits: Cover © Alf Jacob Nilsen/age fotostock; pp. 4-5, 5 (inset), 6, 7, 12, 13, 15 (bottom), 19 Shutterstock.com, p. 8 © Biosphoto/Rotman Jeffrey/ Peter Arnold Inc.; p. 9 Stephen Marks/Getty Images; pp. 10-11 Stephen Frink/ Getty Images; p. 14 © www.iStockphoto.com/George Clerk; p. 15 (top) © www. iStockphoto.com/Mikhail Matsonashvili; pp. 16-17 © K.Aitken/age fotostock; p. 18 © Carson Ganci/age fotostock; p. 20 © www.iStockphoto.com/Kathleen & Scott Snowden; p. 21 (top) © www.iStockphoto.com/Erich Ritter; pp. 21 (bottom), 22 (bottom) © www.iStockphoto.com/Jello5700; p. 22 (top) © www. iStockphoto.com/Ian Scott.

Library of Congress Cataloging-in-Publication Data

Clark, Willow.
 Shark! / by Willow Clark.
     p. cm. — (Animal danger zone)
 Includes index.
 ISBN 978-1-60754-957-4 (library binding) — ISBN 978-1-60754-964-2 (pbk.) — ISBN 978-1-60754-965-9 (6-pack)
 1. Sharks—Juvenile literature. 2. Shark attacks—Juvenile literature. I. Title.
 QL638.9.C535 2010
 597.3—dc22
                                     2010004429

Manufactured in the United States of America

For more great fiction and nonfiction, go to windmillbooks.com.

CPSIA Compliance Information: Batch #S10W: For further information contact Windmill Books, New York, New York at 1-866-478-0556.

TABLE OF CONTENTS

Big, Old Fish

Sharks are large fish that live in every ocean and sea in the world. Sharks are masters at hunting and killing **prey**. There are more than 350 **species** of shark.

Did you know that sharks and their relatives have been around since the time of the dinosaurs? Scientists have found the remains of sharks or shark-like animals that are more than 400 million years old!

Scientists have found shark skeletons that are hundreds of millions of years old. Today's sharks are not much different than their ancient relatives.

Bull sharks have been found in the Mississippi River as far north as Illinois. This is thousands of miles (km) from salt water!

A few species of shark even move between freshwater and salt water. Bull sharks are known to swim into the freshwater of the Mississippi River from the salt water of the Gulf of Mexico.

Sharks are found in all parts of the world's oceans and seas. Great white sharks live near the water's surface. Angel sharks live near the ocean floor. Tiger sharks live in warm waters, while dogfish sharks live in cooler waters.

Like all fish, sharks breathe using **gills**. They use their fins to steer through the water. Unlike other fish, sharks' skeletons are made of **cartilage**, not bone. Cartilage is the same matter that makes up the tip of your nose.

Parts of the cookiecutter shark's body glow in the dark waters of the ocean. This glowing is called bioluminescence.

The whale shark is the world's biggest shark. All sharks are covered with rough skin that feels like sandpaper.

Sharks come in all sizes. The spined pygmy shark only grows to about 7 inches (18 cm) long. The whale shark can be up to 40 feet (12 m) long and weigh 20 tons (18 t)!

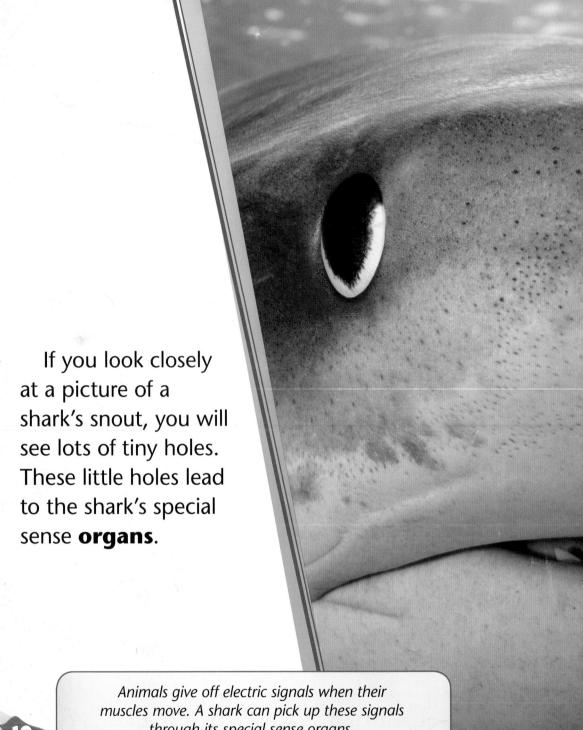

If you look closely at a picture of a shark's snout, you will see lots of tiny holes. These little holes lead to the shark's special sense **organs**.

Animals give off electric signals when their muscles move. A shark can pick up these signals through its special sense organs.

These special sense organs pick up the electric signals that living animals give off. That means a shark can tell if an animal is nearby, even if it doesn't see it! All of a shark's senses are strong, but this special sense helps sharks to be good hunters.

Shark Teeth

When people think of sharks, they often think of their teeth. A great white shark has hundreds of teeth. Each of these teeth can be more than 2.5 inches (5.7 cm) long.

Shark teeth are lined up in rows inside the jaw. Most sharks have about five rows of teeth.

A shark's teeth are closely spaced and knife-like. They are lined up in rows in the shark's jaw. When the teeth in the front row wear down or break off, new teeth move in from behind. Sharks can go through 30,000 teeth in a lifetime!

Sharks are **predators** that eat fish, sea turtles, dolphins, seals, and even other sharks. The tiger shark will eat anything it finds, even garbage. This has earned it the nickname "trash can of the sea!"

Sharks kill their prey by biting them. Instead of chewing their food, however, they swallow large pieces whole.

Sharks eat by tearing off pieces of their prey and swallowing them whole. After eating an animal as big as a seal, a great white shark can go up to a month or two without another big meal.

Sharks hunt prey in many ways. Some use their speed to catch prey. Others **filter** small animals through their teeth. Some sharks hunt alone. Some sharks hunt in groups.

The whale shark swims with its mouth open and filters animals through its teeth. Great white sharks catch their prey by surprise.

The great white shark catches its prey by surprise. It sits underwater. When it senses an animal near the surface, the shark quickly bursts to the surface. It then bites the animal and drags it underwater to eat it.

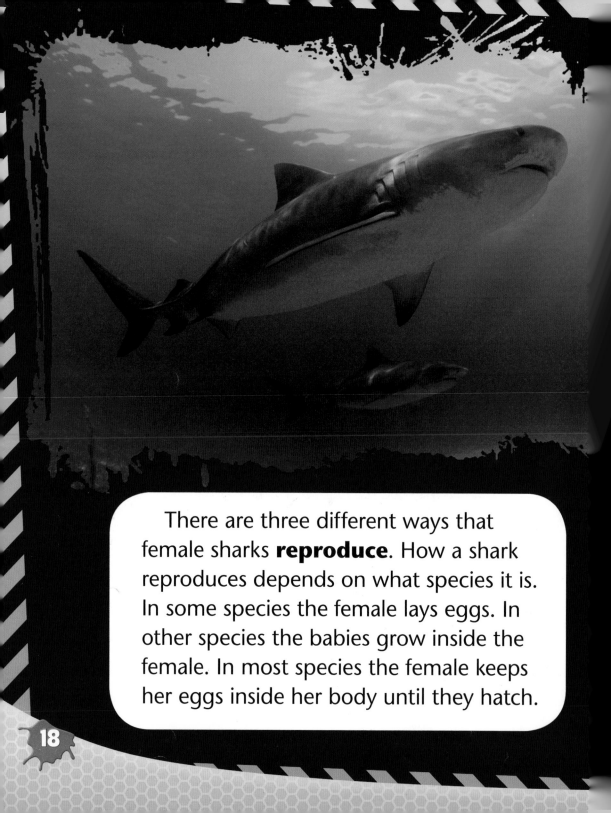

There are three different ways that female sharks **reproduce**. How a shark reproduces depends on what species it is. In some species the female lays eggs. In other species the babies grow inside the female. In most species the female keeps her eggs inside her body until they hatch.

As soon as they are born, baby sharks swim off on their own. Most of them will not live to adulthood because many animals eat baby sharks.

Baby sharks are called pups. Pups are eaten by many animals, even their own mothers!

Shark Attack!

There are about 100 shark attacks each year worldwide. These attacks usually cause serious **injuries**, but do not kill the person.

> Bull sharks are considered the most dangerous sharks to people. This woman has a scar from where a bull shark bit her.

Sharks can mistake a surfer on a surfboard for an animal that it wants to eat.

WARNING

SHARKS SIGHTED

Scientists think shark attacks happen when the shark mistakes a person for an animal that it eats. The shark often swims away when it discovers its mistake. In general, shark attacks are uncommon. Of course, this is not comforting news to a person who has been bitten!

Did You Know?

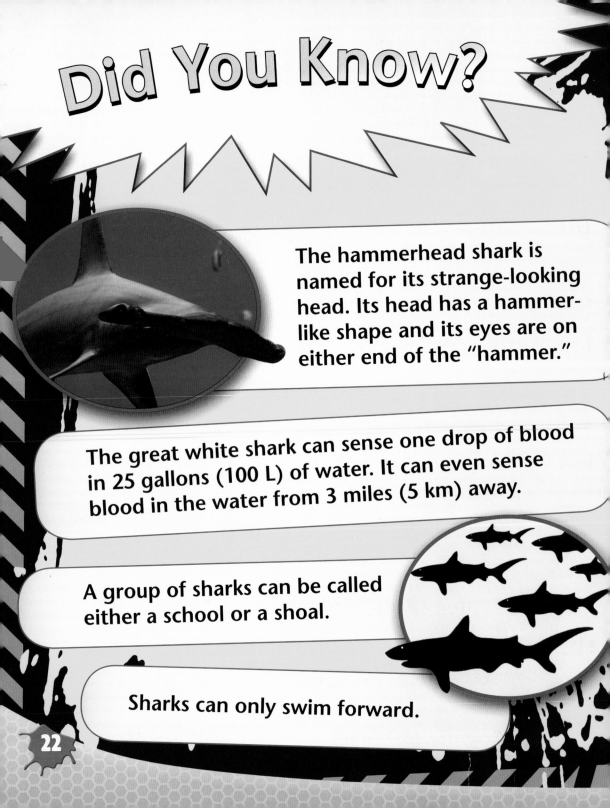

The hammerhead shark is named for its strange-looking head. Its head has a hammer-like shape and its eyes are on either end of the "hammer."

The great white shark can sense one drop of blood in 25 gallons (100 L) of water. It can even sense blood in the water from 3 miles (5 km) away.

A group of sharks can be called either a school or a shoal.

Sharks can only swim forward.

GLOSSARY

cartilage (KAHR-tuh-lij) The bendable matter from which a shark's skeleton made.

filter (FIL-tur) Something that separates wanted things from unwanted things.

gills (GILZ) Body parts that fish use for breathing.

injuries (IN-juh-reez) Hurt done to a person's body.

predator (PREH-duh-ter) An animal that kills other animals for food.

prey (PRAY) An animal that is hunted by another animal for food.

organs (OR-genz) Parts inside the body that do a job.

reproduce (ree-pruh-DOOS) To have babies.

species (SPEE-sheez) One kind of living thing. All people are one species.

Index

Read More

Arnosky, Jim. *All About Sharks*. New York: Scholastic, 2008.

Llewellyn, Claire. *The Best Book of Sharks*. New York: Kingfisher Books, 2005.

Wagner, Kathi. *Everything Kids' Sharks Book: Dive Into Fun-infested Waters!* Cincinnati, OH: Adams Media, 2005.

Web Sites

For Web resources related to the subject of this book, go to: www.windmillbooks.com/weblinks and select this book's title.